WANDERING THE WORLD WITH ASD

Travis Breeding

Travis Breeding

CONTENTS

INTRODUCTION

Welcome to my autobiographical journey of traveling the country to teach people about autism. As someone who has been diagnosed with autism myself, I understand the importance of raising awareness and acceptance of this condition.

Before we begin, let's define what autism spectrum disorder (ASD) is. This is a neurological disorder that affects the way a person communicates, interacts with others, and processes sensory information. It's characterized by difficulty with communication, social interaction, and repetitive behaviors. Individuals with ASD may also have difficulty with motor skills, vision, hearing, and language.

At the age of 22, after years of being isolated and feeling like something was wrong with me, I finally received a diagnosis of autism. This was a huge relief as it gave me a name for my condition and gave me the resources and understanding I needed to start learning more about myself and how to live my best life.

As I continued to learn more about ASD, I began to realize the vast misconceptions and lack of acceptance that exists in the world. This motivated me to start my journey of traveling the country to help teach people about autism.

In this book, I will discuss my experiences of traveling the country for the last five years. I will talk about the people I've met and the places I've seen, and how I've used my story to help educate and create change. I will also talk about the challenges I have faced along the way and the lessons I have learned. Finally, I will provide insight into how I have used my own experience with autism to help raise awareness and acceptance of this condition.

CHAPTER ONE TRAVELING THE COUNTRY WITH AUTISM: PRE-TRIP CHECKLIST, MAKING A PACKING LIST, AND RESEARCHING THE DESTINATION

Traveling is an exciting adventure, especially when you are traveling with autism. For families with members who have autism, the thought of taking a vacation can be daunting. But it doesn't have to be. With a bit of preparation and research, you can ensure a safe and enjoyable trip for everyone involved. Here are some key tips to help you make the most of your travel experience.

Pre-Trip Checklist

Before you begin the process of planning a trip, it is important to consider the needs of those who will be traveling with you. One of the best ways to do this is to create a pre-trip checklist. This is a simple but effective tool for ensuring that all of the necessary preparations are made prior to departure.

The first step on your pre-trip checklist should be to make sure that everyone who is traveling with you has the necessary identification documents such as a passport or driver's license. Additionally, you should make sure that all immunizations and health records are up to date and that any necessary medications are packed.

Another important step in the pre-trip checklist is to research the destination. This includes researching the cultural customs, language, and climate of the area. It is also important to research the accessibility of the destination for those with special needs. This includes researching the availability of ramps, elevators, wheelchair accessible bathrooms, and other accommodations.

It is also a good idea to research the medical care available at the destination. This includes researching the availability of doctors and hospitals that can provide care for those with special needs. Additionally, you should research any medical insurance coverage that may be needed in the event of an emergency.

Finally, it is important to research the transportation options available at your destination. This includes researching the types of transportation available (e.g., public transportation, taxis, etc.), the costs involved, and the safety of the transportation. It is also important to research the availability of special accommodations such as wheelchair lifts or secure seating arrangements.

Making a Packing List

Once the pre-trip checklist is complete, it is time to start making a packing list. This is a great way to ensure that all of the necessary items are packed and to avoid over-packing.

When making a packing list, it is important to consider the needs of those who will be traveling with you. For those with special needs, there may be some items that need to be included in the packing list. For example, special dietary needs may require specialized food items to be packed. Additionally, there may be some medical items that need to be packed, such as medications and medical supplies.

It is also a good idea to consider packing items that may make the trip more enjoyable for those with special needs. These items may include noise-canceling headphones, weighted blankets, and other items that can help create a calming environment. Additionally, it is important to pack any necessary communication devices and/or assistive technology that is needed.

Finally, it is important to pack items that can make travel more comfortable. This includes items such as eyeglasses, extra clothing, travel pillows, and headphones.

Additionally, it is important to pack items that can provide distraction during long periods of travel, such as books, toys, and games.

Researching the Destination

Once the pre-trip checklist and packing list are complete, the next step is to research the destination. When researching the destination, it is important to consider the needs of those traveling with you.

It is important to research the accessibility of the destination. This includes researching the availability of ramps, elevators, wheelchair accessible bathrooms, and other accommodations. Additionally, it is important to research the availability of activities that are appropriate for those with special needs. This includes researching the availability of sensory friendly activities, as well as activities that are specifically designed for those with special needs.

It is also important to research the availability of medical care at the destination. This includes researching the availability of doctors and hospitals that can provide care for those with special needs, as well as researching the availability of medical insurance coverage that may be needed in the event of an emergency.

Additionally, it is important to research the transportation options available at the destination. This includes researching the types of transportation available (e.g., public transportation, taxis, etc.), the costs involved, and the safety of the transportation. It is also important to research the availability of special accommodations such as wheelchair lifts or secure seating arrangements.

Finally, it is important to research the cultural customs, language, and climate of the area. This is important in order to ensure that everyone is respectful of the local customs and comfortable with the climate. Additionally, researching the language of the area can help to reduce the chances of misunderstandings and ensure that communication is as easy as possible.

Conclusion

Traveling with autism can be a challenging experience, but it doesn't have to be. With a bit of preparation and research, you can ensure a safe and enjoyable trip for everyone involved. A pre-trip checklist and packing list are essential tools for ensuring that all of the necessary preparations are made prior to departure. Additionally, researching the destination can help to reduce the chances of misunderstandings and ensure that the trip is as safe and enjoyable as possible. By following these simple steps, you can ensure that your trip is a success.

CHAPTER 2: IDENTIFYING, COPING, AND MINDFULNESS

Traveling with autism can be a daunting task, and understanding and coping with the associated anxiety can seem impossible. Fear not, because with the right mindset and preparation, it can be a manageable and even enjoyable experience. In this chapter, we will discuss how to identify anxiety triggers, find healthy coping mechanisms, and implement mindfulness techniques to help manage anxiety while traveling with autism.

Identifying Anxiety Triggers

The first step in managing anxiety while traveling with autism is to identify the triggers that can cause it. Though every person and situation is different, there are some common triggers that are associated with sensory overload, lack of security and comfort, and unfamiliarity with surroundings.

Sensory Overload: One of the most common triggers of anxiety for people with autism is sensory overload. This can include loud noises, bright lights, cramped spaces, and too much stimulation in the environment. It is important to be aware of the sensory triggers in the environment, identify those that may be particularly difficult, and plan accordingly. It may also be helpful to practice mindfulness techniques during the trip to help manage the stress associated with sensory overload.

Lack of Security and Comfort: Traveling can be uncomfortable and unfamiliar, which can often lead to feelings of insecurity. This can be especially true for individuals with autism, as they may be unfamiliar with the environment and routines. To help make the experience more comfortable, it is important to familiarize oneself with the surroundings prior to the trip and bring comfort items, such as favorite stuffed animals, books, and games.

Unfamiliarity with Surroundings: Traveling to unfamiliar places can be intimidating for anyone, but it can be especially difficult for individuals with autism who may be unfamiliar with the environment and the people in it. To help make the experience less overwhelming, it is important to learn about the area ahead of time, plan out the trip, and stick to a routine as much as possible.

Finding Healthy Coping Mechanisms

Once the triggers have been identified, the next step is to find healthy coping mechanisms to help manage the anxiety. Though it may seem impossible, there are many strategies that can be used to help cope with anxiety while traveling with autism.

Stimulation Strategies: One of the most effective ways to manage anxiety while traveling is to use stimulation strategies. These strategies involve engaging in activities that can help distract the mind and reduce stress. Examples of these activities include listening to music, watching movies, playing video games, or engaging in conversation with other people.

Deep Breathing Exercises: Another useful coping mechanism for managing anxiety is deep breathing exercises. Deep breathing exercises can help reduce stress by slowing down the heart rate and calming the nervous system. It is important to remember to take slow, deep breaths, and to focus on the breath and the body while doing so.

Routine: Routines can be incredibly helpful for managing anxiety while traveling, as they can provide a sense of security and familiarity. Creating a daily routine can help to structure the day and provide structure and predictability. It is important to remember to be flexible with the routine, as some days may require more structure than others.

Implementing Mindfulness Techniques

Once the triggers have been identified and healthy coping mechanisms have been established, the next step is to implement mindfulness techniques to help manage anxiety while traveling with autism. Mindfulness involves focusing on the present moment and being aware of one's thoughts and feelings. It can be a powerful tool for managing anxiety while traveling, as it helps to stay grounded in the present moment and reduce stress.

Mindful Breathing: Mindful breathing is a simple and effective way to stay present and reduce stress. To practice mindful breathing, it is important to focus on the sensation of breathing and the physical sensations associated with it. It is important to remember to breathe slowly and deeply, and to stay focused on the breath.

Mindful Walking: Mindful walking can be a great way to stay grounded in the present moment and reduce stress. To practice mindful walking, it is important to focus on the physical sensations of walking, such as the sensation of the feet on the ground, the movement of the body, and the sound of the environment. It can be helpful to practice mindful walking for a few minutes each day.

Mindful Eating: Mindful eating is another great way to stay present and reduce stress. To practice mindful eating, it is important to focus on the smell, taste, and texture of the food, as well as the sensations associated with eating it. It is also important to be mindful of one's hunger and fullness cues, and to honor them.

Conclusion

Managing anxiety while traveling with autism can be a challenging task, but with the right mindset and preparation it can be a manageable and even enjoyable experience. By identifying the triggers that can cause anxiety, finding healthy coping mechanisms, and implementing mindfulness techniques, it is possible to manage anxiety while traveling with autism. With the right strategies, traveling with autism can be a rewarding experience.

CHAPTER 3: FLYING WITH AUTISM

Flying with autism can be a difficult and overwhelming experience for many families, especially when it comes to making reservations, navigating the airport, and dealing with flight anxiety. However, with the right preparation and research, flying with autism can be a positive and enjoyable experience for everyone involved.

Making Reservations

Making reservations for a flight when traveling with autism can be a challenging experience. It's important to discuss the flight details with your child and ensure they understand what to expect. You may also want to consider booking a larger seat for them to ensure they feel comfortable and have enough space. Additionally, you should research the airline and its policies to ensure they are autism-friendly.

When making reservations, you should also consider researching the airports you will be flying in and out of. Some airports may be more accommodating for those with autism, such as those that are quieter and less busy. You should also inquire about pre-check-in and pre-boarding options to make the process as stress-free as possible.

You should also consider researching and booking accommodations with autism in mind. This includes researching hotels and attractions that are autism-friendly and will make your experience more enjoyable. You should also consider the possibility of booking a private room or suite if available.

Navigating the Airport

Navigating the airport can be an especially challenging experience for those with autism. To ensure a smooth and stress-free experience, it's important to make sure you and your child are well-prepared. This includes researching and discussing the airport layout and procedures before arriving.

You should also plan to arrive at the airport early to account for any delays and allow yourself enough time to get to check-in, go through security, and board your flight. If available, you should consider taking advantage of pre-check-in and pre-boarding options to make the process as easy as possible.

It's also important to make sure you and your child are prepared for the airport security process. You should check with the TSA and your airline to find out what items are allowed and what items are prohibited. Additionally, you may want to consider bringing along your child's doctor's note or a medical alert tag to help explain any special needs or conditions.

Dealing With Flight Anxiety

For those with autism, flying can be an especially stressful experience. It's important to make sure you and your child are well-prepared and have all their needs met in order to ensure a safe and stress-free flight. This includes preparing a bag with any essentials they may need during the flight and packing snacks and activities they can enjoy.

It's also important to talk to your child about their experience and any concerns they may have before the flight. You should also explain the process to them and make sure they understand what to expect. Additionally, you may want to consider bringing along items that will help them feel comfortable and relaxed, such as noise-canceling headphones, blankets, and pillows.

It's also important to be prepared for any emergency situations during the flight. You should make sure you understand the emergency procedures and have a plan in place for how to handle them. If your child is especially anxious during the flight, you may want to consider talking to the flight crew and asking for accommodations to help them feel comfortable.

Conclusion

Flying with autism can be a difficult and overwhelming experience for many families. However, with the right preparation and research, flying with autism can be a positive and enjoyable experience for everyone involved. It's important to make sure you and your child are well-prepared, understand the process, and have all their needs met in order to ensure a safe and stress-free flight.

CHAPTER 4: HOTEL SELECTION, FINDING ACCESSIBLE OPTIONS, AND ADJUSTING

For those traveling with autism, finding the right accommodations can make all the difference in the overall experience. Understanding what hotel options are available, how to determine if they are suitable for those with autism, and making adjustments to ensure the comfort and safety of everyone involved is essential for a successful trip.

When it comes to choosing a hotel for an autistic traveler, the options can seem overwhelming. It is important to take into account the specific needs of the individual, the budget, and the location. What may be suitable for one may not be for another. Exploring options and reading reviews to ensure the hotel is suitable for everyone's needs is a must before making a booking.

There are numerous aspects to consider when selecting a hotel for an autistic traveler, such as noise levels, accessibility, amenities, and staff. It is important to research restaurants, attractions, and activities nearby that may be of interest. Depending on the individual's needs, a hotel may be chosen based on its proximity to activities, the availability of sensory-friendly rooms, or the ability to accommodate special dietary needs.

Finding Accessible Options

When looking for accessible options, there are several ways to make sure the accommodations are suitable for an autistic traveler. A great place to start is by searching for hotels that are certified as Autism Vacation Ready, which means they have gone through an autism-specific training program. These hotels are more likely to have a better understanding of the needs of an autistic traveler and are more likely to have staff who can make accommodations and adjustments if necessary.

It is also important to ask specific questions when searching for a hotel. Does the hotel have a quiet zone or sensory-friendly room? Are there staff members with special autism training available? Are there accessible menus, or can special dietary requests be accommodated? Can the staff provide assistance with any additional needs?

Making Adjustments

Once the hotel is booked, there are still adjustments that can be made to ensure the comfort and safety of the autistic traveler. It is important to discuss the needs of the individual with the hotel staff prior to arrival. This could include a request to place a 'do not disturb' sign on the door, a request for a more private room, or a request for noise-cancelling headphones or earplugs.

It is also a good idea to discuss any special dietary needs and any sensory items that may be needed. For example, a weighted blanket, noise cancelling headphones, or a sensory box. If the hotel can not accommodate these items, they may be able to provide suggestions for where to purchase them nearby.

In addition, the staff may be able to provide assistance with navigating the hotel. This could include a tour of the hotel to familiarize the traveler with the layout, a discussion of the hotel rules and regulations, or assistance with ordering room service.

Conclusion

Finding a suitable hotel for an autistic traveler can be a daunting task. However, by understanding the needs of the individual, researching the hotel options, and making adjustments to ensure the comfort and safety of the traveler, it can be done. By taking the time to ensure the accommodations are suitable, the overall travel experience will be much more enjoyable for everyone involved.

CHAPTER 5
ACCESSIBLE TRANSPORTATION

The key to successful travel for anyone - but especially for an individual with autism who may require accommodations - is to assess the travel needs and make reservations accordingly. Moreover, having an understanding of various modes of transportation and being able to adapt to them is of the utmost importance.

Assessing Transportation Needs

Prior to beginning any journey, one must assess their transportation needs. For someone with autism, this can be a daunting task. However, with adequate preparation and forethought, it can be made manageable.

When assessing transportation needs, it is important to take into consideration the type of travel and the mode of transportation. Is the travel to be local, or is it to include multiple stops? Is it a one-way trip, or a round trip? Will the traveler be traveling alone, or with companions?

It is also important to consider the actual travel arrangements. Will the traveler require the use of a wheelchair, or any other assistive device? Will the transportation require accessible entrances, or will a special lift be necessary?

These are just a few of the questions that one must take into consideration when assessing their transportation needs.

Making Reservations

Once the traveler has an understanding of their transportation needs, the next step is to make the necessary reservations. Depending on the type of transportation, this can be done in a variety of ways.

For air travel, most airlines offer online booking. This can be done through their website or by calling their customer service representatives. When booking online, it is important to remember to make any special requests, such as wheelchair assistance, accessible seating, etc.

For train travel, one can typically book tickets online or by visiting the train station. It is important to remember to make any special requests, such as wheelchair assistance, accessible seating, etc.

For bus travel, one must typically make reservations through the company's website or by visiting their office. It is important to remember to make any special requests, such as wheelchair assistance, accessible seating, etc.

For car travel, one should make reservations through their local rental agency. It is important to remember to make any special requests, such as wheelchair assistance, accessible seating, etc.

Adapting to Various Modes of Transportation

Once the necessary reservations have been made, the next step is to adapt to various modes of transportation. For someone with autism, this can be especially difficult. However, with adequate preparation and understanding of the environment, it can be made manageable.

When traveling by air, it is important to keep in mind the various security measures in place. It is recommended to arrive early to allow ample time for these procedures. It is also important to give yourself plenty of time to adjust to the new environment - planes can be loud and uncomfortable, and it is important to take some time to acclimate.

When traveling by train, it is important to be aware of the different types of trains and the individual rules and regulations associated with them. It is also important to be aware of one's surroundings and any potential safety concerns.

When traveling by bus, it is important to be aware of the different types of buses and the individual rules and regulations associated with them. It is also important to be aware of one's surroundings and any potential safety concerns.

When traveling by car, it is important to be aware of the rules of the road, as well as any potential safety concerns. It is also important to be aware of the various road conditions and traffic patterns in the area.

In summary, when traveling with autism, it is important to assess one's transportation needs, make the necessary reservations, and adapt to various modes of transportation. With adequate preparation and forethought, travel can be made manageable and enjoyable.

CHAPTER 6
EXPLORING THE
DESTINATION

When traveling the country with autism, planning a sightseeing itinerary is essential. As someone with autism, it can be difficult to make decisions and stick to an itinerary. However, it is important to have a plan in place to ensure that the trip stays on track and everyone remains safe.

The first step in planning a sightseeing itinerary is to decide on a destination. This could include a city, a park, a beach, or any other location that is of interest. Once the destination is chosen, it is important to research the area and find out what attractions it has to offer. Some destinations may require a bit of exploration to find the best sightseeing spots. Google Maps, TripAdvisor, and local tourist boards can be helpful in finding the best places to visit.

After researching the destination, the next step is to create an itinerary that includes all of the attractions that have been identified. It is important to include a variety of activities, such as educational sites, historical sites, and outdoor activities, to ensure that everyone has something to do. It is also important to leave some extra time in the itinerary for spontaneous activities or unexpected delays.

Once the itinerary is complete, it is important to find out which attractions are disability friendly. Many destinations have attractions that are specifically designed to be accessible to people with disabilities, such as wheelchair ramps and audio tours. Additionally, there are many websites that provide information about disability friendly attractions.

Finally, it is important to research any potential accessibility challenges that may be encountered at the destination. Many attractions may not have ramps or elevators, which can make it difficult for people with disabilities to access them. Additionally, some attractions may only be accessible during certain times of the day or require advanced reservations. It is important to research these items ahead of time to ensure that the sightseeing trip is not hindered by unexpected challenges.

Navigating accessibility challenges when traveling the country with autism can be difficult, but it is important to be prepared. With some research and planning ahead of time, it is possible to have a successful and enjoyable sightseeing trip. By researching destinations, creating an itinerary, and researching disability friendly attractions and accessibility challenges, it is possible to have a successful and enjoyable experience when traveling with autism.

CHAPTER 7
MEAL PLANNING AND MANAGING EATING OUT

Meal planning and managing eating out can be a daunting task. Eating outside of the home can feel overwhelming, but with the right preparation, it can be a positive and enjoyable experience. This chapter will discuss the importance of meal planning, choosing a restaurant, and managing food allergies.

Meal Planning

Meal planning is a great way to stay on track with your dietary goals. Knowing what you are going to eat for the week can help you save time and money, reduce stress, and make sure you are eating healthy and delicious meals. Meal planning can also help you stay on track with your goals around eating out.

Planning out when you will eat out can help you avoid making a last-minute decision and prevent you from veering off your established diet. Meal planning also helps you know when and how often you can afford to eat out. By deciding which days you will have meals at home and which days you will eat out, you can better anticipate the cost of eating out and choose a restaurant that fits your budget.

When planning meals for the week, consider what type of restaurant you want to visit. Do you want a quick, casual meal or a more formal sit-down experience? If you are looking for something more casual, then think about fast-casual or fast food restaurants. If you want something a bit more special, then consider a mid-level restaurant or a fine dining experience. Once you decide on the type of restaurant you want to visit, then you can begin to narrow down your selection.

Choosing a Restaurant

Choosing a restaurant can be an exciting process. Start by deciding what type of cuisine you want to experience. You can opt for something familiar and comforting, or try something new and exciting. You can also consider special dietary restrictions, such as vegan, vegetarian, gluten-free, and dairy-free. If you are not sure what type of cuisine you are in the mood for, then you can browse restaurant reviews and menus online to get a better sense of the options available.

Once you have narrowed down your list of restaurants, then you can consider the atmosphere and price range. Do you want a cozy, intimate setting or a more lively atmosphere? Do you want to splurge on a luxurious experience, or do you prefer to stay within a certain budget? Knowing the answers to these questions can help you narrow down your selection of restaurants.

You can also consider the convenience of the restaurant's location. If you are planning an outing with friends or family, then you might want to choose a restaurant that is close to where you all live. If you are traveling, then you may want to choose a restaurant that is near the hotel or other attractions you plan to visit.

Managing Food Allergies

If you or someone in your party has food allergies, then it is important to take extra precautions when choosing a restaurant. You should inform the restaurant ahead of time about any dietary restrictions and ask them for menu items that are suitable for those restrictions. It is also a good idea to double check the ingredients of each dish with the server and the chef to make sure that the dish is safe for the person with allergies.

If in doubt, you can always ask the restaurant to make a custom-made dish that is tailored to the person's dietary needs. This can be a great way to enjoy a delicious meal without worrying about potential allergens. Additionally, you can always ask the restaurant if they are willing to prepare the food in a separate area, such as a dedicated fryer or cooking station, to further reduce the risk of cross-contamination.

Conclusion

Meal planning, choosing a restaurant, and managing food

allergies can help you have a positive and enjoyable experience when dining out. With the right preparation and knowledge, you can enjoy delicious and nutritious meals that suit your dietary needs and budget. By making sure you are informed and prepared, you can maximize your enjoyment of eating out.

CHAPTER 8
PREPARING MY PRESENTATION

The United States is an expansive region, made up of 50 states, all of which have their own unique culture and history. As an individual traveling the country, it is essential to be aware of the different public opinions on a given subject. When it comes to presenting on autism, it is important to research the area in which one is presenting in order to ensure that the material is appropriate for the audience. In this chapter, I will discuss the steps I take to research my audience, prepare my presentations, and practice my talks in order to present them in a professional manner.

Before I begin traveling the United States to present on autism, I research the area in which I am presenting. I use a variety of methods and resources to obtain information about the state, including government websites, local media outlets, and autism-specific organizations. By doing so, I gain a better understanding of the local culture and public opinion on the subject of autism. For example, if I am presenting in the state of Texas, I might research the state's websites, local news outlets, and autism-related organizations, such as Texas Autism Action. All of this information allows me to better prepare for my presentation and tailor it to my audience.

Once I have gained an understanding of my audience, I begin to prepare my presentation. This involves creating a PowerPoint slideshow with engaging visuals and concise descriptions. I also include interactive activities and opportunities for audience participation, as this helps to keep the audience engaged and interested in the material. I always make sure to properly cite my sources, as this allows my audience to further explore the topics discussed in my presentation. Additionally, I include a variety of resources for my audience, such as books, websites, and online support groups.

When I am ready to present, I make sure to practice my talk in order to make it as professional as possible. I create an outline using the PowerPoint slides, and I practice my presentation several times in order to make sure I am comfortable speaking in front of a crowd. I also take time to make sure I am dressed appropriately for the occasion and my audience. For example, if I am presenting at a school, I might wear a suit in order to appear professional, but if I am presenting at a local library, I might opt for a more casual look.

When I present on autism, I always strive to make sure the talk is engaging, informative, and professional. Researching my audience, preparing my presentation, and practicing my talk are key components to achieving these goals. By being aware of the local culture, preparing an engaging PowerPoint, and practicing my presentation, I am able to ensure that my presentations exceed the expectations of my audience.

Ultimately, presenting on autism is a rewarding experience. I am able to share my knowledge and experiences with people across the United States and spread awareness about the subject. By following these basic steps, I am able to present my talks in a professional and engaging manner, no matter what state I am in.

CHAPTER 9
REFLECTING ON MY TRIP TO PRESENT AT AN AUTISM CONFERENCE: EXAMINING MY ACCOMPLISHMENTS, PROCESSING DIFFICULT MOMENTS, AND ADJUSTING FOR FUTURE TRIPS

My trip to present at an autism conference was both an incredibly exciting and incredibly daunting undertaking. On the one hand, I was honored to be invited to present my research and findings on the subject of autism to a group of experts in the field. On the other hand, I felt a tremendous amount of pressure to deliver a presentation that would demonstrate my knowledge and capabilities as a researcher. As I reflect on the trip, I find myself looking back on the accomplishments I achieved, the difficult moments I experienced, and how I used the information I gained to make adjustments for how I handle future trips.

Accomplishments

At the end of the trip, I find myself basking in a sense of accomplishment. My presentation was well-received and I was able to effectively convey my message to the attendees. My slides were designed in a visually pleasing way and I received a number of compliments on their presentation. I also found a lot of benefit in attending the various sessions and workshops offered at the conference. I was able to gain an even better understanding of the research being done on autism and the challenges that those living with the condition face. I also made a number of valuable connections with some of the leading experts in the autism field.

I was also very proud of the work I was able to do in the community while I was there. I was able to visit a number of local organizations that support those living with autism and their families. I was able to have meaningful discussions with members of these organizations and learn more about the services they provide and the challenges they face. I was incredibly moved by the work they do and vowed to use my platform to continue to support the work they do.

Processing Difficult Moments

While I did experience a great deal of success on the trip, there were moments that were more challenging for me. For example, I found myself feeling very anxious and overwhelmed at times. I was fearful that I wouldn't be able to effectively communicate my message or that I wouldn't be able to manage my nerves. I also felt a great deal of pressure to make sure that I was representing my research in a positive light.

When I felt these moments of anxiety and overwhelm, I found it very helpful to take a moment to step back and recognize the progress I had already made. I took a few moments each day to reflect on the successes I had already achieved and the relationships I had built. This gave me the time and space to process my emotions and to remind myself that I was capable and strong.

Adjusting for Future Trips

While the trip was a great success, I also recognize the importance of using the information I gained to make adjustments for how I handle future trips. I now have a better understanding of how to manage my nerves and anxiety. I plan to practice mindfulness and meditation prior to future presenting engagements and to remind myself that I am capable and strong. I also plan to be more mindful of the various ways I can help support the work of the organizations I visit while on the trip. I hope to use my platform to help raise awareness and support for their efforts.

Finally, I plan to continue to build upon the relationships I have already made in the autism field. I hope to use these connections to continue to learn and grow as a researcher and to have a greater impact on the lives of those living with autism.

In conclusion, my trip to present at an autism conference was an incredibly rewarding experience. I am incredibly proud of the work I was able to accomplish and the relationships I was able to build. I also recognize the importance of having a plan for how to manage the difficult moments that I experienced and for how to use the information I gained to make adjustments for future trips. I am confident that by continuing to focus on my accomplishments, process difficult moments, and adjust for future trips, I will be able to make an ever-greater impact on the field of autism research.

CHAPTER 10
CONCLUSION

My journey over the past few months traveling the country to present on autism has been an incredible experience. I have learned so much about myself, my capabilities, and the world around me. I have learned how to prepare for travel, how to overcome my anxiety and fly with autism, how to request accommodations, explore my destination, manage eating out, successfully present on autism, and reflect on my trip. The most important lesson I have learned is that I can travel the country successfully as an autistic person, and that I can do anything I set my mind to.

I prepared for my trip by researching the destination and finding accessible and affordable transportation and accommodations. I also made sure to bring enough supplies, such as snacks and sensory items, to help me feel safe and comfortable. I overcame my anxiety by focusing on the positives, such as the opportunity to explore a new city and meet new people. I also made sure to travel with my support person and request any accommodations necessary to ensure a safe and comfortable travel experience.

Once I arrived to my destination, I explored the city by taking advantage of accessible transportation, such as accessible shuttles and Uber. I also made sure to plan my excursions ahead of time, and to bring snacks to manage my sensory needs. I experienced so much joy and satisfaction from exploring the city and seeing all the sights and attractions.

I managed my eating out by researching restaurants and eateries ahead of time and looking for sensory-friendly options. I also made sure to bring food with me, just in case I did not find the right option. I also made sure to ask for any accommodations necessary to make it easier for me to eat, such as taking away bright lights or providing me with a quieter setting.

I successfully presented on autism by keeping the audience engaged, using visuals and interactive activities to keep their attention, and by allowing enough time for questions and answers at the end. I also made sure to present in an accessible way by using language and visuals that are easy to understand and relate to.

Finally, I reflected on my trip by taking time to think about all the things I learned and all the things I could have done differently. I also spent time thinking about how the trip changed me and how it will have a long-lasting positive effect on my life.

My journey traveling the country to present on autism has been one of the most rewarding experiences of my life. I learned so much about myself and my capabilities and I am now more confident to take on new challenges and travel to new places. Even though traveling as an autistic person can be difficult, it is definitely worth it in the end.

For anyone thinking of traveling the country as an autistic person, my advice to you is to focus on the positives, plan ahead, and request any accommodations you need. Make sure to bring enough supplies and snacks to manage your sensory needs and don't be afraid to ask for help when you need it. Finally, remember to take time to reflect on your trip and all the amazing things you have achieved and experienced.

Traveling the country as an autistic person can be a daunting task, but with the right preparation and mindset, it is completely possible. I hope my story has inspired you to take on this challenge and to discover all the amazing things that traveling has to offer.

APPENDIX

The following appendix provides information on key terms related to Autism Spectrum Disorder and Applied Behavior Analysis that are discussed throughout this book. Each key term has been defined, followed by a description of how the term might be generalized and applied in different contexts.

ABA (Applied Behavior Analysis): Applied Behavior Analysis (ABA) is the use of scientific principles to help change behavior within a specific context. This can include both positive and negative reinforcement, as well as shaping behaviors. ABA can be generalized and applied in a variety of contexts, such as education, therapy, and social/behavioral change. For instance, in the educational realm, ABA can be used to shape student behaviors in the classroom, helping them to learn more effectively and increase social interactions with their peers. In the case of therapy, ABA can be used to help individuals with Autism Spectrum Disorder (ASD) increase their social skills, engage in positive behavior, and learn communication skills. Lastly, ABA can be used in social/behavioral change contexts to help individuals, groups, and communities develop more positive and beneficial behaviors.

Reinforcement: Reinforcement is an intervention technique used in ABA that involves reinforcing desired behaviors with rewards or acknowledgements. Reinforcement can be further divided into two subcategories: positive reinforcement, which involves providing rewards or acknowledgements for desired behaviors, and negative reinforcement, which involves removing or decreasing an aversive stimulus in response to a desired behavior. Reinforcement can be generalized and applied in various contexts, such as education, work, therapy, and parenting. For instance, in the educational realm, it can be used to increase the likelihood of students engaging in desired behaviors, such as following the classroom rules, completing their assignments, and participating in class discussions. In the case of work, reinforcement can be used to increase motivation and performance levels. In the case of therapy, reinforcement can be used to increase the likelihood of desired behaviors and decrease the likelihood of undesired behaviors. Lastly, in the case of parenting, reinforcement can be used to increase positive behavior and decrease negative behavior.

Discrete Trial Training: Discrete Trial Training (DTT) is a type of intervention that involves breaking down complex tasks into smaller, more manageable components and teaching the individual each of these components separately. DTT can be generalized and applied in a variety of contexts. For instance, in the educational realm, it can be used to help students learn new skills or information, such as math or reading. In the case of therapy, DTT can be used to help individuals with Autism Spectrum Disorder learn communication and social skills. Lastly, DTT can be used in the workplace to teach employees new job-related skills.

Prompts: Prompts are intervention techniques used in ABA that involve providing assistance or guidance to the individual in order to help them complete a task. Prompts can be verbal or physical, and can range from simple prompts like verbal encouragement to more complex prompts like physical assistance. Prompts can be generalized and applied in various contexts, such as education, therapy, and the workplace. For instance, in the educational realm, prompts can be used to help students understand and complete assignments. In the case of therapy, prompts can be used to help individuals with ASD learn communication and social skills. Lastly, in the workplace, prompts can be used to teach employees new job-related skills.

Shaping: Shaping is an intervention technique used in ABA that involves gradually reinforcing increasingly close approximations of the desired behavior until the individual is able to complete the task independently. Shaping can be generalized and applied in a variety of contexts, such as education, therapy, and the workplace. For instance, in the educational realm, it can be used to help students learn new skills or information, such as math or reading. In the case of therapy, shaping can be used to help individuals with Autism Spectrum Disorder learn communication and social skills. Lastly, shaping can be used in the workplace to teach employees new job-related skills.

Extinction: Extinction is an intervention technique used

in ABA that involves ignoring or not reinforcing undesired behaviors, which will ultimately lead to the reduction or elimination of those behaviors. Extinction can be generalized and applied in various contexts, such as education, therapy, and parenting. For instance, in the educational realm, extinction can be used to reduce disruptive behaviors in the classroom. In the case of therapy, extinction can be used to reduce undesired behaviors, such as aggression or self-injurious behavior. Lastly, in the case of parenting, extinction can be used to reduce negative behaviors, such as hitting or tantrums.

Generalization: Generalization is the process of transferring skills learned in one context to a different context. It is an important part of ABA intervention, as it allows the individual to apply the skills they have learned in one context to other contexts. Generalization can be generalized and applied in a variety of contexts, such as education, therapy, and the workplace. For instance, in the educational realm, generalization can be used to help students transfer knowledge and skills learned in one class to other classes. In the case of therapy, generalization can be used to help individuals with Autism Spectrum Disorder apply communication and social skills learned in one setting to other settings. Lastly, in the workplace, generalization can be used to help employees apply job-related skills learned in one context to other contexts.

Fading: Fading is an intervention technique used in ABA that involves gradually reducing or eliminating prompts and supports while reinforcing desired behaviors. Fading can be generalized and applied in various contexts, such as education, therapy, and the workplace. For instance, in the educational realm, fading can be used to reduce the amount of guidance and support provided to students while still reinforcing desired behaviors. In the case of therapy, fading can be used to reduce the amount of assistance provided to individuals with Autism Spectrum Disorder while still reinforcing desired behaviors. Lastly, in the workplace, fading can be used to reduce the amount of prompts and assistance provided to employees while still reinforcing desired behaviors.

Errorless Learning: Errorless learning is an intervention technique used in ABA that involves teaching desired behaviors without the individual making mistakes. It is important to note that errorless learning does not mean the individual will never make mistakes, but rather that mistakes are minimized or eliminated. Errorless learning can be generalized and applied in various contexts, such as education, therapy, and the workplace. For instance, in the educational realm, errorless learning can be used to help students learn new skills or information without making mistakes. In the case of therapy, errorless learning can be used to help individuals with Autism Spectrum Disorder learn communication and social skills without making mistakes. Lastly, in the workplace, errorless learning can be used to teach employees new job-related skills without making mistakes.

Discrimination Training: Discrimination training is an intervention technique used in ABA that involves teaching the individual the difference between two or more stimuli. Discrimination training can be generalized and applied in various contexts, such as education, therapy, and the workplace. For instance, in the educational realm, discrimination training can be used to help students distinguish between different colors, shapes, or sizes. In the case of therapy, discrimination training can be used to help individuals with Autism Spectrum Disorder distinguish between different facial expressions or emotions. Lastly, in the workplace, discrimination training can be used to help employees distinguish between different job-related tasks or concepts.

Model/Imitation: Modeling/imitation is an intervention technique used in ABA that involves providing a model for the individual to observe, imitate, and learn from. Modeling/imitation can be generalized and applied in various contexts, such as education, therapy, and the workplace. For instance, in the educational realm, modeling/imitation can be used to help students learn new skills or information, such as math or reading. In the case of therapy, modeling/imitation can be used to help individuals with Autism Spectrum Disorder learn communication and social skills. Lastly, in the workplace, modeling/imitation can be used to help employees learn new job-related skills.

ABOUT THE AUTHOR

Travis Breeding

Travis is author of over 20 books on autism and mental health. Travis hopes to raise awareness and acceptance of neurodivergent individuals. Travis disseminates the science of applied behavior analysis in ways that are relatedable to all.

BOOKS BY THIS AUTHOR

Nature Versus Nurture In Aba: The Tale Of Discrete Tiral Training And Natural Envionrment Teaching

"Nature vs. Nurture in ABA: The Tale of Discrete Trial Training and Natural Environment Teaching" is a comprehensive exploration of the ongoing debate within the field of Applied Behavior Analysis (ABA) regarding the most effective methods of teaching and behavior modification. This book delves into the contrasting approaches of discrete trial training and natural environment teaching, examining their respective strengths and limitations. Through a careful analysis of current research and practical case studies, the book provides insight into the role of both nature and nurture in shaping behavior and offers guidance for practitioners seeking to incorporate evidence-based practices into their work. Whether you are a seasoned ABA professional or a student just entering the field, this book is a must-read for anyone interested in the latest developments in ABA and the ongoing nature vs. nurture debate.

Breaking The Mold: Empowering Autistic Adults In The Workplace

Breaking the Mold" explores the unique challenges and strengths of autistic adults in the workplace. Through a collection of personal stories and expert insights, this book sheds light on the obstacles faced by the autistic community and provides practical strategies for empowering individuals on the spectrum to reach their full potential in their careers. This empowering guide is a must-read for anyone looking to promote diversity, inclusiveness, and understanding in the workplace. Whether you are an autistic adult seeking guidance, an ally looking to support the community, or an HR professional striving to create a more neurodiverse workplace, this book will provide valuable insights and inspiration to help you break the mold and unleash the full potential of autistic adults in the workplace.

I'm Not Unlikeable: I Just Operate On A Different Set Of Rules

Do you know someone living with autism who has struggled to find acceptance and understanding? If so, I'm Not Unlikeable, I Just Operate on a Different Set of Rules may be the book for them. This intriguing autobiography by Travis Breeding is about one autistic adult's life journey, from being undiagnosed until age 22, to then discovering the underlying cause behind his relational and social struggles—autism!

Travis Breeding dives deep into his extraordinary story —one filled with immense personal transformation. He reveals how his journey led him to come to terms with multiple comorbid conditions, such as anxiety, depression, misdiagnosis of schizoaffective disorder in 2013 at age 28 and inappropriate social boundaries making it challenging to effectively manage communication and relationships.

Through adversity and hope comes great recovery – this book tells the passionate story that leads up to Travis' goal of applying Behavior Analysis techniques to help others have more meaningful lives. A highly recommended read for anyone who wants to explore what it's like for an autistic adult navigating through uncertain times and gaining new insight into living their best life possible!

Practical Solution To Practical Problems: An Autistic View Of Applied Behavior Analysis

Applied behavior analysis is a field of psychology that deals with the modification of behavior. It is one of the few interventions that has been shown to be effective with individuals on the autism spectrum. This book is geared towards practitioners who wish to learn more about the advanced topics related to applied behavior analysis. It discusses social validity, medical necessity, pragmatic language, generalization and application of social skills, and dosage amounts of applied behavior analysis to be provided to individuals with autism spectrum disorder.

www.ingramcontent.com/pod-product-compliance
Lightning Source LLC
Chambersburg PA
CBHW051707250726
48653CB00007B/2898